MOTIVATIONAL JOURNEY

QUOTES

BY CARLINE BAKER

Copyright

Motivational Journey
Copyright © 2023 by Carline Baker

First Edition

Pure Thoughts Publishing, LLC

Brief news excerpts, public statements, and images by individuals or companies other than the author are used under section 107 of the copyright act 1976; allowance is made for "fair use" for purposes such as criticism, commentary, news reporting, teaching, scholarship, and research.
No part of this book may be reproduced in whole or in part, stored in a retrieval system, or transmitted in any form, or by any means, electronic, mechanical, photocopying, recording, or otherwise, without prior permission of the author, except by a reviewer, who may quote brief passages in a review.

ISBN: 978-1-953760-30-2
All rights reserved.

This Book Belongs To

_____

MOTIVATIONAL JOURNEY

QUOTES

MOTIVATIONAL JOURNEY

> **ONLY EXPECT OF OTHERS WHAT YOU EXPECT OF YOURSELF**

MOTIVATIONAL JOURNEY

MOTIVATIONAL JOURNEY

> "LIFE MIGHT HAVE A FEW DETOURS
> BUT SOMETIMES
> THAT'S HOW YOU GET TO WHERE
> YOU NEED TO GO"

MOTIVATIONAL JOURNEY

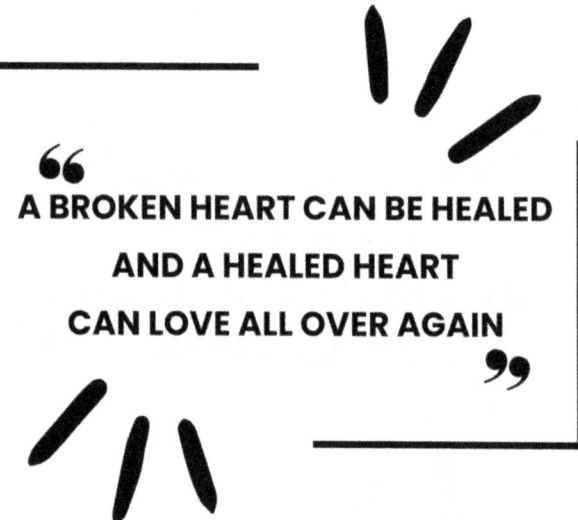

"A BROKEN HEART CAN BE HEALED AND A HEALED HEART CAN LOVE ALL OVER AGAIN"

MOTIVATIONAL JOURNEY

> **NO ONE IS BETTER THAN YOU BUT YOU ARE BETTER THAN NO ONE**

MOTIVATIONAL JOURNEY

MOTIVATIONAL JOURNEY

> **LIFE IS A JOURNEY
> NOT EVERYONE GETS
> TO GO ON IT WITH YOU**

MOTIVATIONAL JOURNEY

> "WE CANNOT CORRECT YESTERDAY
> WE CAN ONLY TRY
> TO MAKE TOMORROW BETTER"

MOTIVATIONAL JOURNEY

> **LIVE YOUR WAY TOWARDS RETIREMENT
> DO NOT WORK TOWARDS IT**

MOTIVATIONAL JOURNEY

> **I'D RATHER HAVE HONESTY OVER PRAISES**

MOTIVATIONAL JOURNEY

> "DON'T ASK ME TO SEE THOUGH YOUR EYES
> I CAN ONLY SEE THOUGH *MINE*"

MOTIVATIONAL JOURNEY

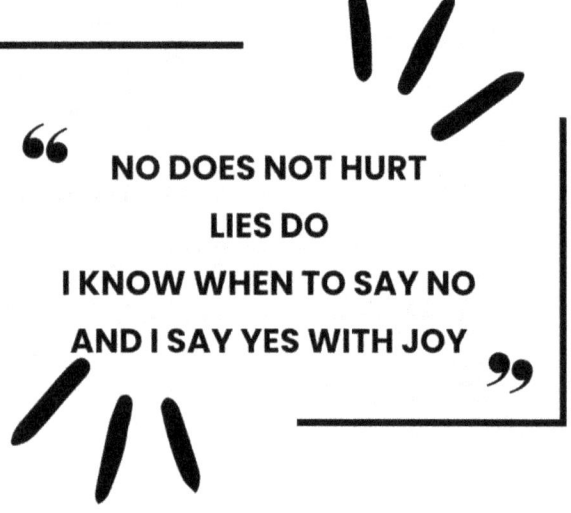

"NO DOES NOT HURT
LIES DO
I KNOW WHEN TO SAY NO
AND I SAY YES WITH JOY"

MOTIVATIONAL JOURNEY

> **SOMETIMES THE WHATS ARE NOT AS IMPORTANT AS THE WHYS**

MOTIVATIONAL JOURNEY

> **LIFE GIVES YOU A LEMON MAKE LEMONAIDE AND INVITE SOME FRIENDS**

MOTIVATIONAL JOURNEY

MOTIVATIONAL JOURNEY

> "**YOU HAVE EVERYTHING YOU NEED FOR TODAY
> YOU WILL ONLY SEE IT IF YOU STOP LOOKING FOR YOUR YESTERDAY AND TOMORROW**"

MOTIVATIONAL JOURNEY

> "
> **WHAT YOU DO TODAY
> IS MORE IMPORTANT
> THAN WHAT YOU DO TOMORROW**
> "

MOTIVATIONAL JOURNEY

**I KNOW I AM NOT PERFECT
BUT I LOVE WHO I AM**

MOTIVATIONAL JOURNEY

"
**NO IS AN ANSWER TOO
IT'S OK TO USE IT**
"

MOTIVATIONAL JOURNEY

> **ALLOW ME TO LOVE ME
> SO I CAN LOVE YOU**

MOTIVATIONAL JOURNEY

> **YOU DON'T HAVE TO UNDERSTAND
> I AM THE ONE FEELING IT**

MOTIVATIONAL JOURNEY

> **SOMETIMES THE EARS ARE MORE IMPORTANT THAN THE OPINIONS**

MOTIVATIONAL JOURNEY

> **CALL ME SELFISH
> I TURN THE WE INTO ME**

MOTIVATIONAL JOURNEY

> **"SOMETIMES WE NEED TO LOVE FROM A DISTANCE FREEDOM COMES WHEN YOU LEARN TO LET GO"**

MOTIVATIONAL JOURNEY

> **THINGS AND PEOPLE
> WE LOVE ARE NEVER FAR AWAY**

MOTIVATIONAL JOURNEY

> "
> **CHOOSE TO SEE THE GLASS
> HALF FULL
> THEN YOU WILL ALWAYS
> HAVE SOMETHING TO DRINK**
> "

MOTIVATIONAL JOURNEY

> "AS WE FOCUS ON WHO WE WERE
> WE GET TO CHOOSE WHO
> WE WANT TO BE NEXT"

MOTIVATIONAL JOURNEY

> A SMILE A DAY KEEPS THE WRINKLES AWAY

MOTIVATIONAL JOURNEY

> "GRATITUDE IS THE HABIT
> OF ENJOYING WHAT YOU HAVE
> WHILE YOU HAVE IT"

MOTIVATIONAL JOURNEY

> **PEOPLE ARE LIKE LEAVES
> THEY WILL NOT STAY WITH YOU
> FOREVER
> SOME WILL FALL
> SOME YOU HAVE TO CUT OFF
> SOME THE WIND WILL TAKE AWAY**

MOTIVATIONAL JOURNEY

> **THE WORLD IS UNIQUE BECAUSE WE ALL MAKE IT UP**

MOTIVATIONAL JOURNEY

> **PEOPLE ALREADY PERCIEVE YOU TO BE WHO THEY WANT YOU TO BE SO JUST BE YOURSELF**

MOTIVATIONAL JOURNEY

> "
>
> **PEOPLE DON'T DISAPPOINT US OUR EXPECTATIONS OF THEM ARE TOO HIGH**
>
> "

MOTIVATIONAL JOURNEY

> **SOME OF LIFE'S EXPERIENCES CANNOT BE PUT ON YOUR RESUME BUT YOU STILL HAVE THEM**

MOTIVATIONAL JOURNEY

> **"**
>
> **NEVER SETTLE FOR LESS THAN
> YOUR DREAMS
> SOME WHERE SOME TIME
> SOME DAY SOME HOW
> YOU WILL HAVE THEM**
>
> **"**

MOTIVATIONAL JOURNEY

> **THE COAL ONLY BECOMES THE DIAMOND AFTER THE PROCESS**

MOTIVATIONAL JOURNEY

> **EXPERIENCES ARE THE FERTILIZER FOR LIFE'S GROWTH**

MOTIVATIONAL JOURNEY

> **WHEN YOU REACH THE BOTTOM THERE IS NOWHERETO GO BUT UP**

MOTIVATIONAL JOURNEY

> **PEOPLE TEACHES YOU HOW TO TREAT THEM MAKE SURE YOU LEARN**

MOTIVATIONAL JOURNEY

> "
> **IT TAKES MORE ENERGY TO HOLD ON TO THINGS AND PEOPLE WHO ARE TRYING TO GO**
> "

MOTIVATIONAL JOURNEY

> "IT'S NOT THE HOURS YOU PUT INTO
> THE WORK THAT COUNTS
> IT'S THE WORK
> YOU PUT INTO THE HOURS"

MOTIVATIONAL JOURNEY

> **DO NOT BE AFRAID
> OF YOUR ENEMIES
> BE AFRAID OF YOUR FRIENDS**

MOTIVATIONAL JOURNEY

> **LEARN HOW TO LOVE
> THE UNLOVABLES
> THAT GOD PLACE IN YOUR LIFE**

MOTIVATIONAL JOURNEY

> **IT IS BETTER TO HAVE LOVED
> AND LOST
> THAN NEVER LOVED AT ALL**

MOTIVATIONAL JOURNEY

> **IF YOU ONLY READ
> THE COVER OF THE BOOK
> YOU CANNOT TELL THE
> WHOLE STORY**

MOTIVATIONAL JOURNEY

> **DON'T THINK YOU KNOW ME FROM WHAT YOU SEE ING ON THE OUTSIDE**

MOTIVATIONAL JOURNEY

> **IT'S OK TO LOOK IN YOUR REAR VEIW MIRROR OF LIFE JUST DON'T KEEP STARING IN IT WHILE GOING FORWARD**

MOTIVATIONAL JOURNEY

> **GRATITUDE
> IS TURNING WHAT YOU HAVE
> INTO ENOUGH**

MOTIVATIONAL JOURNEY

> **THE STARS SHINES BRIGHTER IN THE DARK**

MOTIVATIONAL JOURNEY

> **LET YOUR LIGHT SHINE
> LET NOTHING OR NO ONE
> DIM IT**

MOTIVATIONAL JOURNEY

> **YOU CAN FEEL OLD AT TWENTY
> YOU CAN FEEL YOUNG AT EIGHTY
> YOU MAKE THE CHOICE**

MOTIVATIONAL JOURNEY

> **AGE IS JUST A NUMBER
> GIVE THE NUMBER NO POWER OVER
> WHAT YOU CAN OR CANNOT DO**

MOTIVATIONAL JOURNEY

> **AGE IS JUST A NUMBER ALLOW THE NUMBER TO GO AS HIGH AS IT WANTS TO WHILE YOU RELAX AND ENJOY THE RIDE**

MOTIVATIONAL JOURNEY

> **THE HIGHER THE NUMER IN AGING**
> **THE MORE EXPERIENCES**
> **THE MORE KNOWLEDGE**
> **YOU HAVE**

MOTIVATIONAL JOURNEY

> **RELATIONSHIPS ARE LIKE
> A BEAUTIFULL BED OF ROSES
> IT COMES WITH THORNS
> AND YOU HAVE TO NOURISH IT
> WHILE FOCUSING ON IT'S BEAUTY**

MOTIVATIONAL JOURNEY

> **YOU WERE BORN COMPLETE
> YOU NEED NOTHING OR NO ONE
> TO COMPLETE YOU
> KNOW WHO YOU ARE
> ACCEPT WHO YOU ARE
> THEN YOU WILL SEE YOURSELF**

MOTIVATIONAL JOURNEY

> "DON'T STOP PRAYING
> FOR PRAY WE MUST
> BUT HAVE MORE TRUST THAT GOD
> ANSWERS PRAYER
> THE APPRECIATION OF THE VALLEY
> IS ON THE MOUNTAIN TOP"

MOTIVATIONAL JOURNEY

> **THE APPRECIATION OF THE CANDLE IS IN THE DARKNESS**

MOTIVATIONAL JOURNEY

> **LIFE IS FOR LIVING
> NOT JUST EXISTING**

MOTIVATIONAL JOURNEY

> **FAILURE IS AN APPOTUNITY TO TRY AGAIN**

MOTIVATIONAL JOURNEY

> **IT'S BETTER TO TRY AND FAIL THAN TO NEVER TRY**

www.ingramcontent.com/pod-product-compliance
Lightning Source LLC
Chambersburg PA
CBHW060854050426
42453CB00008B/972